Seven Things You Should Know About Divine Healing

Kenneth E. Hagin

Unless otherwise indicated, all Scripture quotations in this volume are from the *King James Version* of the Bible.

Fourth Printing 1983

ISBN 0-89276-400-7

In the U.S. write:
Kenneth Hagin Ministries, Inc.
P.O. Box 50126
Tulsa, Oklahoma 74150

In Canada write:
Kenneth Hagin Ministries
P.O. Box 335
Islington (Toronto), Ontario
Canada, M9A 4X3

BOOKS BY KENNETH E. HAGIN

I Went to Hell
I Believe in Visions
Exceedingly Growing Faith
The Woman Question
New Thresholds of Faith
Prevailing Prayer to Peace
Concerning Spiritual Gifts
Bible Faith Study Course
Bible Prayer Study Course
The Holy Spirit and His Gifts
The Ministry Gifts (Study Guide)
Seven Things You Should Know About Divine Healing
El Shaddai
Zoe: The God-Kind of Life
A Commonsense Guide to Fasting
Must Christians Suffer?
How You Can Be Led By the Spirit of God
What To Do When Faith Seems Weak and Victory Lost
The Name of Jesus
The Art of Intercession
Growing Up, Spiritually
Bodily Healing and The Atonement
Redimido De La Pobreza, La Enfermedad, La Muerte
La Fe, Lo Que Es
Siete Pasos Para Recibir El Espiritu Santo
?Piensa Usted Bien? O Mal?
La Autoridad Del Creyente
Como Desatar Su Fe
La Medicina de Dios

BOOKS BY KENNETH HAGIN JR.

Man's Impossibility—God's Possibility
Because of Jesus
Unity: Key to the Age of Power
Faith Worketh by Love
Blueprint for Building Strong Faith
Seven Hindrances to Healing
The Past Tense of God's Word
Healing: A Forever-Settled Subject
How To Make the Dream God Gave You Come True
Faith Takes Back What the Devil's Stolen
"The Prison Door Is Open — What Are You Still Doing Inside?"
Itching Ears
Where Do We Go From Here?
How To Be A Success in Life

Contents

1. It is God's will to heal you, because healing is in His Redemptive Plan.

Scripture reveals the *nature* of God to us.

Scripture also reveals the *attitude* of God toward sin, sickness, and disease.

God's nature has not changed through the ages. Neither has His attitude changed toward sin, sickness, and disease.

You need to know this in order to understand divine healing. In fact, there are seven principal facts you should know about divine healing. The first is:

1. It is God's will to heal you, because healing is in His redemptive plan.

The Bible says that in the mouth of two or three witnesses every word shall be established (Matt. 18:16). The following texts from Isaiah, Matthew, and First Peter agree that *"Himself* (Jesus) *took our infirmities, and bare our sicknesses."*

> Surely he hath borne our GRIEFS, and carried our SORROWS: yet we did esteem him stricken, smitten of God, and afflicted. But he was wounded for our transgressions, he was bruised for our iniquities: the chastisement of our peace was upon him; and WITH HIS STRIPES WE ARE HEALED.
>
> —Isaiah 53:4,5

This is from the King James translation. A good reference Bible will have a marginal note by the words "griefs" and "sorrows" to tell you that the Hebrew words are literally "sicknesses" and "diseases."

Dr. Isaac Leeser's translation of the Hebrew Bible—a translation authorized for use by Orthodox Jews—reads, "*Our diseases did he bear himself, and our pains he carried: while we indeed esteemed him stricken, smitten of God, and afflicted.*"

> That it might be fulfilled which was spoken by Esaias the prophet, saying, HIMSELF TOOK OUR INFIRMITIES, AND BARE OUR SICKNESSES.
>
> —Matthew 8:17

This is clearer yet. Matthew says he is quoting Isaiah. If you check the reference, you will find he is quoting Isaiah 53:4. I like to say it this way: "Jesus took *my* infirmities and bare *my* sicknesses."

I read that verse for years before I understood what it was saying: Jesus actually—literally—took the *cause* of our sickness and disease. He took our infirmities and bare our sicknesses.

We know that Jesus was made to be sin for us. The object of His sin-bearing was that we might be free from sin, and the object of his sickness-bearing was that we might be free from sickness.

> Who his own self bare our sins in his own body on the tree, that we, being dead to sins, should live unto righteousness: by whose stripes YE WERE HEALED.
>
> —1 Peter 2:24

Thus, Isaiah, Matthew, and Peter—three witnesses—tell us that not only did Jesus shed His blood for the remission of our sins, but with His stripes we *were* healed.

Some people do not believe this. I once read a commentary whose author said that *"by whose stripes ye were healed"* (1 Peter

2:24) does not mean physical healing; it means spiritual healing. Your *spirit* is healed by His stripes.

God, however, does not heal the spirit of the sinner. According to Scripture, He *recreates* it and makes the person a new creature.

Jeremiah and Ezekiel, prophesying in the Old Testament, said, *"Behold, the days come, saith the Lord, that I will make a new covenant with the house of Israel...."* (Jer. 31:31); *"... and I will put a new SPIRIT within you; and I will take the stony heart out of their flesh, and will give them an heart of flesh"* (Ezek. 11:19).

Those who believe that God heals man's spirit do not believe that man ever failed (or sinned). Their unscriptural propaganda says that all of us have a spark of divinity that God needs to perfect.

No! A sinner needs to be born again and become a new man—the new creature described in Second Corinthians 5:17: *"Therefore if any man be in Christ, he is a new creature: old things are passed away; behold, all things are become new."* (The marginal note here says that he is a *"new creation."*)

When a person gets *healed*, however, old things do not pass away and all things become new; just the sickness passes away. The part that was diseased becomes new.

(If I have a boil on my nose and that boil gets healed, I don't get a new nose. It's the same nose I had. Just the diseased part is gone.)

Therefore, First Peter 2.24 does not mean spiritual healing; it means just what it said. I thought as I read further from this gentleman's commentary, *If this means spiritual healing, then the Lord Himself did not know it and He made a mistake.* I was recalling an incident that happened during a meeting I held in Oklahoma.

One of the seven cooperating churches was pastored by a couple I had known in Texas. They said, "We're going to bring a woman from our church for prayer one night, Brother Hagin. She is crippled. She has not walked a step in seven years. We have taken her to the best specialists in the state, and they have said she'll never walk again 'the longest day she lives.' "

Ordinarily I minister under the anointing. The night she came, I had so many to minister to that by the time I got to her I was exhausted.

You see, the Lord is the same all the time, but I am not. Potentially, the anointing is there all the time, but in manifestation it is not, because when you grow weary, it is difficult to yield to God.

Because the anointing was gone by the time I got to this woman, I couldn't conscientiously minister to her as I normally would. They had brought her to the meeting from a distance, and what was I to do? Just send her away?

No, no. There was a way to minister to her—because God's Word never fails! The anointing may wane, disappear, and be gone, but the Word of God is anointed forever, hallelujah, and His Words are Spirit and Life.

All I did was sit down on the altar beside the woman, open my Bible to this verse of Scripture (1 Peter 2:24), lay the Bible on her lap, and ask her to read it.

Then I asked her, "Is the Word *were* past tense, future tense, or present tense?"

A look of recognition flashed across her face like a Neon light lighting up in the dark. "Why," she said, "it's past tense. And **if we WERE** healed, **I WAS!**" (That is believing in line with God's Word.)

I said, "Sister, will you do what I tell you to do?"

"Well," she said, "I will if it's easy."

I said, "It's the easiest thing you ever did in your life. Just lift up your hands and start praising God, because you *are* healed—*not going to be*—ARE!"

I wish you could have seen that crippled woman. She had no evidence of healing—she had not yet walked a step—but she lifted her hands, looked up, and as a smile broke across her face, she said, "Oh, dear Father God—whooo! I'm so glad I'm healed! Oh, Lord, you know how tired I got sitting around these last few years. I'm so glad I'm not helpless and don't need to be waited on anymore." (You see, she was acting on the Word. That's what faith is.)

I stood and told the congregation, "Let's all lift our hands and praise God with her, because she *is* healed." (And yet, from all observation, she was still sitting on the altar, crippled.)

After we stopped I turned to the woman and said, *"Now, my sister, rise and walk in Jesus' Name!"*

God and hundreds of people are my eternal witnesses that instantly she leaped to her feet and jumped and ran and danced like the man who went into the Temple walking and leaping and praising God (Acts 3:8).

We all shouted and cried with her. Then somebody went off and told a lie about me! He said, "That fellow Hagin healed a crippled woman over there last night."

I didn't have anymore to do with it than you or anybody else could have.

Jesus healed her nearly 2,000 years ago, and she just found out about it that night!

The point I am making is that although that so-called minister said that First Peter 2:24 does not mean physical healing, this was the only verse I gave the crippled woman!

I thought to myself, *If that verse means only spiritual healing, then God made a mistake. He should have healed her spiritually, not physically!*

Friends, that verse means just what it says, and it belongs to us now. Bless God, by His stripes we *were* healed. He not only redeemed us from sin; He also redeemed us from sickness.

It *is* God's will to heal you. Never doubt it, because it *is* in His redemptive plan.

2. *It is God's will to heal you because sickness comes from Satan, not from God.*

2. It is God's will to heal you because sickness comes from Satan, not from God, and God doesn't want His children to have anything that belongs to Satan.

> How God anointed Jesus of Nazareth with the Holy Ghost and with power: who went about doing good, and healing all that were oppressed of the devil; for God was with him.
>
> —Acts 10:38

I want you to notice that the Scripture said that every one of these sick persons Jesus healed was oppressed of the devil. And do you notice what the Bible calls sickness? Satanic oppression. Jesus is the Deliverer, but Satan is the oppressor.

> (Jesus said) And ought not this woman, being a daughter of Abraham, WHOM SATAN HATH BOUND, lo, these eighteen years, be loosed from this bond on the sabbath day?
>
> —Luke 13:16

If you read the entire story in the 13th chapter of Luke, you will see that this woman evidently had a disease like arthritis,

13

because she could not stand straight. Jesus said that it was Satan who had bound her physical body.

> The thief cometh not, but for to steal, and to kill, and to destroy: I AM COME THAT THEY MIGHT HAVE LIFE, and that they might have it more abundantly.
>
> —John 10:10

When Jesus said, "The *thief* cometh not," He was talking about the devil, not God. God is not a thief. Jesus is not a thief. The Holy Spirit is not a thief.

The thief comes to steal, kill, and destroy. Sickness is a thief. It steals health. It steals happiness. It steals the money we need for other things.

When Jesus said, *"I am come that they might have life, and that they might have it more abundantly,"* He was contrasting His works—the works of God—with the works of the devil.

> He that committeth sin is of the devil; for the devil sinneth from the beginning. FOR THIS PURPOSE THE SON OF GOD WAS MANIFESTED, THAT HE MIGHT DESTROY THE WORKS OF THE DEVIL.
>
> —1 John 3:8

For this purpose—for this reason—the Son of God was manifested: He came that He might destroy the WORKS of the devil!

Yes, sin is of the devil, and Jesus came to *destroy* sin. But that is not all He came to destroy. He also *"went about doing good, and healing all that were oppressed of the devil,"* according to our text from Acts 10:38. You see, Jesus was manifested to destroy the WORKS of the devil. Notice again that this text from Acts calls sickness and disease *the works of the devil.*

When we realize this—when we begin to treat sickness and disease just like we would treat sin and the devil—then we will resist them and not yield to them. Our first mistake is when we yield to them.

I remember how angry I got when the devil tried to attack our children with sickness when they were small. It made me mad for the devil to invade our home and strike those children. I stood against him. I said to him, "You're not going to get in here! You have no right!"

Our children are grown now. Our son, Ken Jr., an ordained minister, is director of RHEMA Bible Training Center. Our daughter, Pat, also an ordained minister, and her husband, Reverend Buddy Harrison, pastor Faith Christian Fellowship in Tulsa.

I tell people all the time that all it ever cost us medically speaking to raise these children was $37.50.

When Ken Jr. was born, the doctor charged $25. That was the total cost in those 1939 Depression days. And when Pat was born, the doctor charged $12.50. (I'd better straighten that out with the girls. We had a different doctor, and he gave pastors a 50 percent discount!)

(Now, do not misunderstand me. When the time came for our children to start school, we took them in for physical examinations and whatever shots the law said they were supposed to have, but the doctor in the town where we were pastoring then did not charge ministers anything.)

Thank God, healing belongs to us. We need to stand against the devil.

3. *God not only provided healing in the Old Testament; He also provided healing in the New Testament.*

3. God not only dealt with sickness and provided healing in the Old Testament under the Old Covenant; He also dealt with sickness and provided healing in the New Testament under the New Covenant.

Most people who have studied the Bible know that God dealt with sickness in the Old Testament. Furthermore, something about the nature of God can be learned from these Old Testament Scriptures.

As soon as Israel, God's covenant people, came out of Egypt and started toward their homeland, God said to them:

> If thou wilt diligently hearken to the voice of the Lord thy God, and wilt do that which is right in his sight, and wilt give ear to his commandments, and keep all his statutes, I will put none of these diseases upon thee, which I have brought upon the Egyptians: for I AM THE LORD THAT HEALETH THEE.
>
> —Exodus 15:26

The Hebrew literally reads "I will *permit* none of these diseases upon thee, which I *permitted* upon the Egyptians . . . . " Notice that God did not put the diseases on Israel or the

17

Egyptians. *It is Satan, the god of this world, who makes men
sick.* Here, Jehovah declares that He is to be Israel's healer. And
then in Exodus the 23rd chapter, God said:

> And ye shall serve the Lord your God, and he shall bless thy bread,
> and thy water; and I WILL TAKE SICKNESS AWAY FROM THE
> MIDST OF THEE. There shall nothing cast their young, nor be
> barren in the land: THE NUMBER OF THY DAYS I WILL
> FULFILL.
>
> —Exodus 23:25,26

A minister once asked this question: "If you are not going to
be *sick*, how are you ever going to *die?*" It tells you right here in
verse 26: *"the number of thy days I will fulfill."*

God had promised He would take sickness from the midst of
them. That means that they just wore out, fell asleep, and went
home, bless God, without sickness.

It is a remarkable fact that as long as Israel walked in the
covenant God made with them, there was no sickness among
them. There is no record of any babies or young people ever
having died as long as Israel kept the covenant. There were no
premature deaths, because every person grew to his full age
before he laid down his work. You see, **Jehovah God was
everything they needed!**

Now, in Deuteronomy the 7th chapter, God said to Israel:

> And he will love thee, and bless thee, and multiply thee: he will
> also bless the fruit of thy womb, and the fruit of thy land, thy corn,
> and thy wine, and thine oil, the increase of thy kine, and the flocks
> of thy sheep, in the land which he sware unto thy fathers to give
> thee. Thou shalt be blessed above all people: there shall not be
> male or female barren among you, or among your cattle. And THE
> LORD WILL TAKE AWAY FROM THEE ALL SICKNESS, and
> will put none of the evil diseases of Egypt, which thou knowest,
> upon thee; but will lay them upon all them that hate thee.
>
> —Deuteronomy 7:13-15

This is talking about how God will love, bless, and multiply
His children. He says He also will bless the fruit of their womb,

the fruit of their land, and the increase of their flocks. That means He will prosper them materially. They will be blessed above all people.

You see, everything connected with the people of God is to bear the stamp of prosperity and success. Sickness and disease are not to be tolerated among them.

Note verse 15: *"And the Lord will take away from thee all sickness—ALL SICKNESS—and will put* (or as the Hebrew says, "permit") *none of the evil diseases of Egypt . . . upon thee."*

In our English Bible, Psalms is one book of 150 chapters. The Hebrew Bible, however, has five books of Psalms, corresponding to the first five books of the Bible. These books of Psalms were Israel's prayer and song books. If you read the Psalms carefully, they continually mention that God is Israel's healer.

One of the most important examples is the 103rd Psalm:

> Who forgiveth all thine iniquities; WHO HEALETH ALL THY DISEASES. Who redeemeth thy life from destruction; who crowneth thee with lovingkindness and tender mercies; Who satisfieth thy mouth with good things; so that thy youth is renewed like the eagle's.
>
> —Psalm 103:3-5

The fact that disease came through Israel's disobedience to the law of God is evident. Forgiveness for their disobedience meant the healing of their bodies. Let me repeat that: *Forgiveness for their disobedience meant the healing of their bodies.*

Did God say here, "Who forgiveth *all* thine iniquities; who healeth *half* of thy diseases—or *all but one?"* No! ALL thy diseases" is what it says.

In the 107th Psalm after God told Israel (v. 11) that the reason for their disease and sickness was that they rebelled against the Word of God and condemned the counsel of the Most High, He declared:

> Fools because of their transgression, and because of their iniquities, are afflicted. Their soul abhorreth all manner of meat; and they draw near unto the gates of death. Then they cry unto the

Lord in their trouble, and he saveth them out of their distresses.
HE SENT HIS WORD, AND HEALED THEM, and delivered them
from their destructions.

—Psalm 107:17-20

They're sick. They draw near to the gates of death. Then they
cry to the Lord and He saves them. He sends His Word and heals
them and delivers them.

You see, *they had taken themselves out of the protection of the
Covenant that God made with them.* It had been God's plan that
they live out their full lifespan without sickness or disease.

We can read and rejoice over all these verses, and still some
people will sit around in unbelief and say, "Well, yes, but that is
all in the Old Testament. That is just for Israel."

Let me ask you something: Is God any different now than He
was back then? Has He changed? Is He the same God? If God was
opposed to His people being sick *then*, He is opposed to it *now*—
because God never changes.

Remember, the third most important principle you should
know about healing is that God not only dealt with sickness and
provided healing in the Old Testament; but He also dealt with
sickness and provided healing in the New Testament.

I remember something important Jesus said to me once
when He appeared to me in a vision. He was talking to me about
this very subject, and He said, "Israel were not sons of God."

They never had been born again. They just had a promissory
note on redemption. They were *servants* of God.

And Jesus said to me, *"If God didn't want His **servants** sick,
you know He doesn't want His **sons** sick."* Hallelujah!

In addition, the Bible tells us we have a *better* covenant
established on *better* promises: "he is the mediator of a ***better***
*covenant, which was established upon **better** promises"* (Heb.
8:6).

If divine healing is not provided under this better covenant,
it would not be a "better" covenant.

Under a covenant *not as good as ours*, the children of Israel
had the potential of going through life without sickness or

disease, of never, NEVER being sick, and of living the full length of their allotted years. Under our *better* covenant (the New Covenant), do we have to go through life sick and suffering? It doesn't make sense.

If one covenant is *better* than another, it includes *all* that the other one included and *more*, too, or it's not better. Is a $10 bill better than a $5 bill? Yes! Why? Because it includes all that the $5 bill is and more.

It said in the Old Testament that God sent His Word and healed them. The Word that He sent was spoken through the prophets, but **the Word that He sent to heal in the New Testament is Jesus Christ the Son of God!** This written Word—the New Testament—unveils to us the Living Word and tells us that by His stripes we were healed. He is the healing Word.

> In the beginning was the Word, and the Word was with God, and the Word was God. The same was in the beginning with God. All things were made by him; and without him was not any thing made that was made . . . The Word was made flesh and dwelt among us.
>
> —John 1:1-3,14

Praise God, that was Jesus! He is the Word God sent. Himself took our infirmities, and bare our sicknesses.

I am fully convinced—I would die saying it is so—that it is the plan of Our Father God, in His great love and in His great mercy, that no believer should ever be sick; that every believer should live his full lifespan down here on this earth; and that every believer should finally just fall asleep in Jesus. (He will know when the time comes to go.)

I was baptized with the Holy Spirit and spoke with other tongues in 1937 as a young Baptist pastor. I then received "the left foot of fellowship" from among the Baptists. Eventually, in June 1939, my wife and I accepted the pastorate of a little Full Gospel church in the blackland of northcentral Texas.

One day a woman in our church and I got to talking about the promises of divine healing. This sister had a Methodist background. Her husband was a farmer.

She told me some Pentecostal people had come into that little town about 1918, had rented an empty store building, and had started a revival.

The family heard about it and decided they would attend. They hooked up the wagon, loaded all their children, and went in town to the meeting. They attended a few times and enjoyed it. The preacher was preaching on divine healing and praying for the sick. People were praying around the altar, and all of them prayed out loud at once!

The one member of their household who could not attend was this woman's 93-year-old grandmother. They got home too late at night for her.

One morning at the breakfast table, Grandma asked about the service. "Well, I know you're not going to like this . . . . " the granddaughter said, and began to tell her about the fellow preaching on healing, anointing people with oil, and laying hands on them for healing.

But Grandma exclaimed, "WHOOPEE! Glory! Glory! I'm glad you found it!"

"What do you mean?" her granddaughter asked.

"Why," she said, "40 years ago in our Methodist church a fellow came along preaching divine healing, and he invited us to come up and accept Christ as our Healer and Physician, just as we had accepted Him as our Savior. And I went forward with the others. You're old enough to remember most of those 40 years. Did you ever know of my being sick in the last 40 years?"

"Why, no. We just always thought you had a *strong constitution!*"

"No," the grandmother said. "I accepted Jesus as my Physician. I haven't been sick in 40 years. I'm 93 now—and it might interest you to know that I am going home *without* sickness and disease. I'll never have a sick day in my life!"

The sister said to me, "We thought poor old Grandma had

become sort of senile, but she encouraged us to go to the meetings."

Grandma lived to be past 94. She got up with the rest of the family before daylight, because by daylight the men and boys would be out in the fields working. After breakfast she would always wash and dry the breakfast dishes, clean up the kitchen, and sweep it out while her granddaughter was making the beds and cleaning the rest of the house.

By 9 o'clock they would meet in their sewing room. While the granddaughter mended, Grandma would read the Bible to her.

The sister recalled, "At the breakfast table one morning, Grandma said, 'I'm going home this morning at 10 o'clock.' We passed it by, but before my husband went out to the fields, he said, 'What is she talking about? Does she think she's going back home?' We didn't understand what she meant."

Grandma went ahead and washed all the breakfast dishes and pots and pans that it took to feed eight children plus the three adults, swept out the kitchen, met her granddaughter at 9 o'clock in the sewing room, sat down, and began reading the Bible to her.

Her granddaughter said, "Just about 10 minutes till 10, she turned to me and said, 'Let me read this to you . . . .' She read the 20th and 21st chapters of Revelation. She got through about 10 o'clock, said, 'There's Jesus—and I must go! Goodbye!' waved, and went home, sitting there in a chair."

(And she was Methodist! Bless God, if it would work for a *Methodist,* it ought to work for anybody!)

Oh, hallelujah, we have sold God short so many times.

"Yes, but maybe that's not God's will for *me,*" you might say.

Well, you just go right ahead and talk yourself out of it. Talk yourself into being sick. Talk yourself into dying early—and you will have what you say, because Jesus Himself plainly said:

> That whosoever shall say . . . and shall not doubt in his heart, but shall believe that those things which he saith shall come to pass; he shall have whatsoever he saith.
>
> —Mark 11:23

I'm going to state it again: **It is NOT God our Heavenly Father's will that Christians should suffer with cancer and other dread diseases that bring pain and anguish. It IS God's will that we live our full length of time on earth.**

As long as Israel kept the Old Covenant laws, no illness was among them; but when they sinned, their bodies were filled with disease. They were sick because of broken laws—because of sinning against the Word of God.

But what is so wonderful about it is that even then—when they had sinned and their bodies were filled with disease—they had a right to turn to the Lord and find *forgiveness* for their sins and *healing* for their bodies, because the Bible says, *"Who forgiveth all thine iniquities; who healeth all thy diseases"* (Ps. 103:3).

Is healing in the New Covenant? Come with me to the Book of James in the New Testament.

> Is any sick among you? let him call for the elders of the church; and let them pray over him, anointing him with oil in the name of the Lord.
>
> —James 5:14

Did you notice that there is a question mark at the end of that first sentence? James asked a question: "Is there any sick among you?" You would not write to a church today and say, "Is there any sick among you?" You would just write, " . . . the 85 or 90 percent of you who are sick."

The fact that James asked the question infers there should *not* have been any sick among them. It infers they should have known Matthew 8:17, *"Himself took our infirmities, and bare our sicknesses."* It infers they should have known First Peter 2:24, *"by whose stripes ye were healed."*

But *is* anyone sick among you? Let him call for the elders of the church. What church is that? It is the New Testament Church, of which all born-again believers are a part. Some groups think they are "The Church," but they aren't. They are not the whole sum and total of the Church of Jesus Christ; they are only a part of it.

I will tell you something else. The "early Church" was not really different from the Church today. Christ was the head of The Church then, and He is the head of The Church now. I'm in the same Church they were in.

I was reading where a seminary professor (a fellow with a big education but knowing nothing about the Bible) said that this verse, James 5:14, just belonged to the Jews.

He said that James was addressing the Twelve Tribes scattered abroad. He also said that because God had made a covenant of healing with the Jews, *they* could be healed even under the New Covenant, but *Gentiles* could not, because they never had been included in the covenant.

But it says right here, *"Is any sick among you? let him call for . . . the church."* That poor fellow failed to realize that there are Gentiles in "The Church," for "whosoever will may come." Therefore, healing does not belong exclusively to Jewish believers; it belongs to "The Church."

The Book of Galatians is a letter written to all the churches in Galatia—and these churches were all Gentile churches. The Spirit of God plainly stated through the Apostle Paul:

> Christ hath redeemed us from the curse of the law, being made a curse for us: for it is written, Cursed is every one that hangeth on a tree: That the blessing of Abraham might come on the Gentiles.
> —Galatians 3:13,14

Because one of the curses of the law is sickness, we could paraphrase this verse this way: "Christ has redeemed us from the curse of sickness, being made a curse for us . . . that the blessing of Abraham might come on the Gentiles . . . . " Glory!

When I was studying the Bible as a boy on the bed of sickness and found a good Scripture that offered a possibility of my being healed or given material prosperity, somebody would always say, "That's just for the Jews." I didn't know any better, so I let them put out this light.

Wouldn't it be strange that God would want the Jews to be without sickness—He would want Israel to prosper and be successful—but He would want His Church, that He sent His only begotten Son to die for, to go through life sick and afflicted, in pain and misery, poverty stricken, their nose to the grindstone, living on Barely-Get-Along Street, away down at the end of the block, right next to Grumble Alley? Wouldn't that be strange?

If that were so, then why did Jesus Christ, the Son of God, say, *"If ye then, being evil* (carnal, natural human beings) *know how to give good gifts unto your children, how much more—* HOW MUCH MORE, HOW MUCH MORE, HOW MUCH MORE, HOW MUCH MORE—*shall your Father which is in heaven give good things to them that ask him?"* (Matt. 7:11).

If you had children, would it be your will that your children be sick and afflicted? Certainly not! Would it be your will that they go through life poverty stricken and begging? No, no, no!

Many parents have worked their fingers to the bone to see that their children receive a better education than they had. Why? So life will be easier for them. Because they love them.

Now, do you think God loves us any less? Jesus said He loves us *more.*

Oh, I was so thrilled when I found out about that! I haven't stopped shouting yet.

I was preaching once in a large church in Texas when God dealt with me to preach on Sunday morning. He gave me the message and the text.

I preached on the subject "He Has Redeemed Us from the Curse of Poverty." (There were some of those Sunday morning Christians there whom I never got to preach to at any other time, and I wanted them to find out what belonged to them.)

Then the pastor took me out to Sunday dinner. He sat there and whined and cried and said, "Brother Hagin, I *wish* I could believe that. That sounds good. I *wish* I could believe that God wanted me to have something in this life."

I told him, "Bless God, *I* can believe it! It's in His Book, and He wants me to have what He paid for."

The poor fellow. He never has had anything except sickness, disease, poverty, tragedy, and debt. He wanted to believe it and couldn't. Why couldn't he? He was steeped in religion—brainwashed with religious teaching—instead of being New Testament taught. He could not believe that God is that kind of God; that His Heavenly Father is that kind of a Father. Oh, thank God He is. HE IS. HE IS.

The 53rd chapter of Isaiah gives us a graphic portrait of the coming Messiah, the Lord Jesus Christ. The literal Hebrew translation says:

"He was despised and shunned by men; a man of pains, and acquainted with disease; and as one who hid his face from us was he despised, and we esteemed him not. But only our diseases did he bear himself, and our pains he carried: while we indeed esteemed him stricken, smitten of God, and afflicted. Yet he was wounded for our transgressions, he was bruised for our iniquities: the chastisement for our peace was upon him; and through his bruises was healing granted to us" (Isa. 53:3-6, Leeser).

We are the ones who transgressed. We are the ones who sinned. It should have come on us. These Scriptures have to do with the disease and sin problems that confront the Church and the world today.

You see, *God dealt with man's spirit, soul, and body when He laid our iniquities and diseases upon Jesus.* As Matthew said, *"Himself took our infirmities, and bare our sicknesses"* (Matt. 8:17). That is under this New Covenant—this New Testament. *Healing belongs to us in the New Covenant.*

Now let's go back again to James 5:14,15. *"Is any sick among you? let him call for the elders of the church; and let them pray over him, anointing him with oil in the name of the Lord: And the prayer of faith shall save the sick, and the Lord shall raise him up."*

That is not talking about salvation, because it says "the Lord shall raise him up."

But, wait, that is not all of it! I want to show you something we've missed at the end of verse 15. *"And if he have committed sins, they shall be forgiven him."*

If he has done what?

Committed sins.

I have had people tell me, "The Lord is not going to heal Brother So-and-so. He's sinned. He's done wrong. I know He won't heal him."

Then I prayed for him, and he got healed.

I've had people say, "That fellow Hagin must not be right, because he prayed for this person and got him healed—and I happen to know that he has *sinned*." But did they happen to know he had *repented*?

The mercy of God amazes me.

Years ago, when people whom I thought surely would *not* get healed *did*, and when good church members I was sure *would* get healed but *didn't*, I almost was ready to accuse God and say, "Lord, why did you heal *that* person?"

I was holding a meeting in South Texas at the time our second granddaughter was born. My wife went home to be with our daughter, and I was struggling along. The meeting was just dead for the first week. It was one of the toughest places I had ever been.

About Tuesday night of the second week, the Spirit of God moved on a man. The Word of Knowledge was manifested through him. Some healings took place. Others were used by the Spirit in tongues and interpretation, but God's using this particular man just really set the meeting off.

I said to myself as I sat on the platform, *This is the turning point. From now on this will be like another meeting.* And it was. There was as much difference in the last half and the first as there is between daylight and dark. God blessed immeasurably. Great things happened. I saw people get healed.

I was staying in a little travel trailer. I watched the 10 o'clock news, turned the television off, and went to bed—but something kept bothering me.

You see, I had driven down the main street of that town that very day, and I had seen this man who was so mightily used of God go into a dark dive. When something like that happens, your mind just runs. You think *What is he doing in there?* Then the devil fills in all the blanks for you!

I drove around the block, came back, and he was still in there. I don't know how long he stayed.

So I was lying there trying to go to sleep, and that thought just kept pestering me: *Why did God use that fellow?* Several days before I had heard him say some things that were just not up to par. That kept coming back to me, too.

I struggled for 30 minutes to get off to sleep. (My wife can tell you that I usually go to sleep by the time my head hits the pillow.)

Finally I sat up in bed and said, "All right, Lord! All right! I'm going to ask You: Why did You use that fellow? Didn't You see him go into that dark dive like I did? Didn't You hear what he said, like I did?

"I know that was You tonight. I know the Spirit of God. I know that You revealed things to him, that You worked through him, and that healings took place. I saw them: miracles, right in front of our eyes.

"But, God, why couldn't You have used old Sister So-and-so, 80 years old. She's been in The Way for 50 years almost. She's filled with the Holy Spirit, sanctified, holy, separated . . . Or if You didn't want to use her, why didn't You use (and I mentioned a few others)."

I got it off my chest. I waited for Him to answer. Down inside myself I heard it. It hit me so hard it was like somebody hit me in the stomach with their fist. I grabbed my stomach.

He said, "Your trouble is, you don't believe your own preaching."

I tried to defend myself. I said, "Lord, You've hit me a low blow. Why, I'm a stickler for the Word. I believe the Word."

"No," He said, "you don't."

He said, "You were teaching the other morning in the Bible class from Isaiah 43, where I said, *'I, even I, am he that blotted out thy transgressions for mine own sake, and I will not remember thine iniquities'* " (vv. 25,26).

He said, "You may have seen that fellow go in that place, but you don't know what happened. When he saw what he was getting into, he said, 'Dear God, what's the matter with me? I didn't intend to get into this. Lord, forgive me.' And I didn't remember that he had ever done anything wrong."

(And He didn't remember, did He? You see, *we* remember a person's sins, but God doesn't. How does He keep from it, you ask. I don't know. Go ask Him, if you want to know. I don't want to know; I just believe it.)

He said to me, "You asked why I couldn't use Sister So-and-so. What you don't know about that dear old saint is that she has been in disobedience for 40 years. You can't see that on the outside. I talked to her 40 years ago about doing some things and she wouldn't. She comes to church, lives right, and on the outside looks good. But this man had done wrong and had repented of it. I did not remember that he had ever done anything wrong."

I said, "Thank You, Lord. Just go ahead and use him if You want to. It's all right with me. I'll believe my preaching." I lay down and went to sleep.

You see, people sometimes say, "You know that *couldn't* have been God. That fellow used to be *this*, or that woman used to do *that*. That *couldn't* be God working through them."

But if they have repented, God doesn't remember that they ever did anything wrong!

Can you see that?

Often, people have been robbed of healing that belonged to them because somebody told them, "You've done wrong. You're going to have to pay for it. God's going to hold that against you forever. You're going to have to go through life sick and suffering."

A man in Houston told me, "The doctor said, 'If you stay on your job, you'll fall dead any minute of your heart condition, high blood pressure, kidney disease, and liver trouble.' "

This was back in the 1950s. Every healing evangelist in America had laid hands on this man, and no insinuation, because I had laid hands on him twice, and he hadn't gotten healed.

He said, "In 36 years, I've missed it. Oh, I've missed it so many ways. I've failed. I could have been a better Christian."

I showed him this verse in James: *"The Lord shall raise him up and if they have committed sins . . . . "* (Did you notice it said sins, not sin?)

"What awful sins have you committed in these 36 years?" I asked him. "How many people have you killed?"

"Not any," he said.

"How many banks have you robbed?"

He said, "None."

"Well," I said, "what awful sins *have* you done?"

He said, "Really, I haven't done much as far as sins of commission are concerned. It's sins of omission. I could have done so much more than I did. I could have given more to missions."

I said, "Have you repented?"

"Oh, yes."

"Those sins are forgiven," I said. "Now let Him heal you."

I laid hands on him. He didn't fall dead on the job. He worked until he was 75 years old, and he was still alive the last I heard of him. He had been letting the devil cheat him because he had missed it.

No, I'm not encouraging people to do wrong or sin, but don't let the devil rob you of your healing just because you missed it.

People have asked me, "Brother Hagin, if healing is ours, why don't we have it in our church?" I'll tell you why: because you don't *preach* it in your church.

Although healing belongs to us, and Jesus purchased it for us, it does not fall on us like ripe cherries off a tree. The same is true of salvation.

Did you ever stop to think about it: Jesus did not just die for *us*; He shed His blood, died, and purchased redemption for everybody in the world.

Salvation . . . the New Birth . . . the remission of sins . . .

belongs to the worst prostitute walking the streets of your city just as much as it belongs to you. Why doesn't she have it, then, if it belongs to her?

Because redemption does not "fall" on you. Although it *belongs* to you, you must do something with it. You can either receive it or reject it. You are not a robot. God will not push His blessings off on you.

Jesus said, *"Go ye into all the world, and preach the gospel to every creature. He that believeth and is baptized shall be saved: but he that believeth not shall be damned"* (Mark 16:15,16).

Even after we are born again, we may use our free moral agency. We don't become machines.

I was born and reared a Southern Baptist. I had heard the New Birth preached all my life. I joined the church and was baptized in water at 9 years of age. Many people in the church make the mistake of thinking that joining the church is the New Birth.

On my bed of sickness as a teenager, I came to the realization that I was not saved—had never been saved—and did not know God. Having had salvation preached to me, and knowing that God would forgive me, I cried out to Him in the Name of Jesus.

It was like a two-ton weight rolled off my chest. Peace came in. Really, right then, it did not make any difference to me whether I lived or died; I was so happy.

Why didn't healing "fall" on me if healing was for me? Salvation was all I knew at that point. It was all of the Bible I had ever heard preached. I couldn't believe beyond it.

You see, I had the door shut on God. For lack of a better term—and I say this humbly—God and the Holy Spirit are perfect gentlemen. They will not push in on you.

The devil is not a gentleman. Open the door an inch and he will stick his foot in it. His evil spirits *drive* and *force* people to do things. You see that all through the Bible.

The Holy Spirit never uses force. The Holy Spirit is gentle. You never read where the Holy Spirit *forced* anybody. The Holy Spirit *leads* people: *"As many as are led by the Spirit . . . . "* (Rom. 8:14). The Holy Spirit will *lead* you. It is up to you to *follow.*

I did not know that. Therefore, I was an invalid for 16 long months until I could get into the Word of God and find out what belongs to me.

However, I never doubted—the thought never entered my mind—that the Lord would not forgive me of my sins and save me, cleanse me, and make me a new creature. I don't understand people who doubt their salvation. I never have had a shadow of a doubt about my salvation since being saved the 22nd day of April 1933 in the south bedroom at 405 North College Street in McKinney, Texas.

The devil knew better than to bring that up to me. He knew I would have quickly put him on the run with a few jabs from the Sword of the Spirit, the Word of God.

Gradually I began to see what God's Word says on the subject of divine healing. It took me a long time to see it—16 months—because I had not been taught that divine healing is for today.

Nobody had ever told me that the New Birth had been done away with, but people did tell me that healing and miracles had been done away with.

But I got into the Bible. Thank God for this Book. I can remember those hours, days, weeks, and months bedfast. I used to sleep with the Book in my arms.

After I had been bedfast about a year, I had gotten to the point where I could read all day long if I wanted to. My family got concerned about it. They loved me, but they didn't understand what I was learning. I had begun to talk about some things I had seen in the Bible. They said, "Oh, no! Now, son, that's not for us today."

I kept my own counsel and stayed with the Word. We Baptists had a motto: "The Bible says it, I believe it, and that settles it for me." I wrote in red ink in the fly leaf of my Bible: "The Bible says it, I believe it, and that settles it."

My family asked the doctor to come by. (Doctors still made housecalls in 1934!) I had the Bible spread out on the bed, and was making a few notes when he came.

He said, "I haven't seen you in a long time, and I was out this

way making another call, so I stopped by." I had not known he
was coming, but they didn't have me fooled; I knew my family
had asked him to come.

He checked me over. Then he pointed to the Bible on the bed
and said, "Son, are you reading that much?"

"That's all I do read," I said.

He said, "Do you ever read the funny paper?" (Today they
call it the comic section.)

I said, "No, sir. I don't have time."

I knew he thought I was an idiot. Here I was bedfast 24 hours
a day and I'm saying I didn't have *time* to read the funny paper.
What I meant was, "I'm not going to waste my time reading the
funny paper—not at a time like this."

He said, "Do you ever read the sports page?"

(I do now, but I didn't then.) I said, "No, I never read the
sports page. I don't have time."

"Do you ever read the newspaper?"

I said, "No. Once in a while I'll glance at the headlines if
somebody else is reading the paper in the room. I don't have
time."

He said, "Do you read any novels?"

I said, "No, sir. I don't have time."

"Well," he said. "It's all right to read the Bible, but if you stay
with one thing all the time, you'll become a fanatic!"

I'm glad I did! Praise God, I'm glad I did! I became a fanatic!
I'm still a fanatic after 45 years. That doctor talked to me 45
years ago, and I'm *still* a fanatic.

But I'll tell you one thing: Getting to be a fanatic got rid of
my paralysis for me. It got rid of the incurable blood disease for
me. It got rid of the heart condition for me.

I have had time to read many other things since then, but
books, magazines, and newspapers were not going to bring me
the help I needed when I was sick. I knew what I was seeking
had to be in the Word, so I put the Word first.

And when I saw what the Bible says about healing, the
thought never entered my mind that I might *not* be healed. I

never had a doubt about it. You see, when you get into God's Word, doubts vanish.

If you have doubts, the reason is because you are not yet grounded in the Word. Let God's Word be the final authority— the Supreme Court, so to speak—to which you appeal.

So you see, healing does not fall on people automatically any more than salvation falls on people automatically. Preach the Word. *"Faith cometh by hearing, and hearing by the word of God"* (Rom. 10:17).

A preacher said to me years ago, "I've discovered something. When I only preached salvation, I had a church full of people who were saved—and they had needed to be saved. That's basic. That's the first thing. But not many had the baptism in the Holy Spirit. I couldn't figure it out.

"Then I began to preach the baptism in the Holy Spirit, and they began to get filled with the Spirit—some of them before they could get to the altar; some at home; some driving their cars; some on their way to church. I just kept preaching on it until everybody in the church was baptized in the Holy Spirit.

"Then the thought struck me: *You know, when people ask, I anoint them with oil and lay hands on them for healing, but I don't preach on it.*

"We had not had many people get healed," the pastor said, "so I just started preaching on healing at least once a week. And the moment I started preaching on it, people started getting healed."

That is the way faith comes. *"The entrance of thy words giveth light"* (Ps. 119:130). As we study the Word, we find that healing belongs to us.

4. There are a number of methods in the Word whereby healings can be obtained.

4. There are a number of methods in the Word whereby healings can be obtained.

Because everybody's faith is not on the same level, God has provided seven methods by which physical healings can be obtained through the Word of God. God does not leave us stranded. If we cannot rise to meet Him on His level, He will come down to meet us on ours.

(1) Use the Name of Jesus against the devil. Demand in the Name of Jesus that the disease and sickness leave.

> And whatsoever ye shall ASK in my name, that will I do, that the Father may be glorified in the Son. If ye shall ASK any thing in my name, I will do it.
> —John 14:13,14

Jesus is not talking about prayer in these verses. (He *was* talking about prayer in John 16:23, when He said, "*Whatsoever ye shall ask the Father in my name, he will give it you.*" That is a prayer.)

The word "ask" in these verses actually has the stronger meaning of "demand" in the original Greek. Jesus said,

37

"Whatever you ask—whatever you *demand*—in my Name, I will do."

All through the Acts of the Apostles, the apostles did not *pray* for the sick; they *demanded* that they get up and walk. When Peter and John ministered to the lame man at the Gate Beautiful (Acts 3), they "demanded" in the Name of Jesus (it says in the Greek), that he rise and walk.

You have a right to "demand" in the Name of Jesus that people be healed. You are not demanding it of God; He did not make them sick in the first place. You are demanding that the devil turn them loose in the Name of Jesus.

Jesus said, *"IN MY NAME they shall lay hands on the sick, and they shall recover"* (Mark 16:17,18). "IN MY NAME they will do it." Hallelujah, there is power in the Name.

I notice that when I get down to basics in dealing with demons, I say to them, "I demand my rights in the Name of Jesus!"—and they take off like they were shot. They are afraid of that Name because Jesus defeated them. He made a show of them openly, the Bible says (Colossians 2:15).

Another thing you can do is take the Name of Jesus to break the power of the devil over your loved ones' lives. No, you cannot *make* them accept Christ—but you can make it *easier* for them to accept Christ by doing this.

Many of us who were reared in church were religiously brainwashed instead of New Testament taught. Sometimes I find myself reverting back to prayer practices I was taught in church. Praying about something day after day and night after night, suddenly I realize: *Wait a minute! I know better than that! That's not the way to pray. That won't work. That's not Bible. That's just religious junk!*

So I simply say: "I demand my rights in the Name of Jesus!" I'm demanding it of the devil. Jesus told me to use His name.

Let's know what belongs to us. Let's know that the Name of Jesus belongs to us in this generation just as much as it did to the first-century Christians. Praise God, we have a right to use that Name.

There is just as much power in the Name of Jesus as there was in Jesus when He was here on earth.

There is healing in that Name.

There is deliverance in that Name.

That Name belongs to us, but it will not work unless we use it.

The Name of Jesus is the KEY that unlocks the door to the impossible.

The Name of Jesus is the KEY that unlocks the door to the supernatural.

Not my name. Not your name. His Name.

Remember what Peter said to the crowd that gathered after the lame man was healed at the Gate Beautiful? *"Why marvel ye at this? or why look ye so earnestly on us, as though by our own power or holiness we had made this man to walk?"* (Acts 3:12) They hadn't. They didn't have any power.

"Oh, yes," somebody will say, "but they were *apostles*."

That is what Peter explained. He said, *"faith in his name—* the Name of Jesus*—hath made this man strong . . .* (and) *hath given him this perfect soundness in the presence of you all"* (Acts 3:16).

Glory! Hallelujah! That Name is ours. Let's use it!

(2)   Pray for healing to the Father in the Name of Jesus.

> And IN THAT DAY ye shall ask me nothing. Verily, verily, I say
> unto you, Whatsoever ye shall ask the Father IN MY NAME, he
> will give it you. Hitherto have ye asked nothing IN MY NAME:
> ask, and ye shall receive, that your joy may be full.
> —John 16:23,24

Mark these verses in your Bible. Don't let them get away from you.

When Jesus said "in that day ye shall ask me nothing," what day was He talking about? He was talking about the day that we are living in right now. Praying to the Father in the Name of Jesus belongs to us NOW—in this day.

Jesus said that just before He went to Calvary to die, be raised from the dead, ascend on high, and sit at the right hand of the Father, after which a new day dawned, and we came into the *New Covenant.*

Notice the 24th verse says, *"Hitherto have ye asked nothing in my name."* Hitherto means up until now—until this time— you have not prayed in My Name.

You see, it would not have done the disciples or anybody else any good to have prayed to the Father in the Name of Jesus while Jesus was here on earth, because, under the *Old Covenant,* they prayed to the God of Abraham, Isaac, and Jacob.

Furthermore, when Jesus was here on earth, He had not yet entered into His mediatorial (high priestly or intercessory) ministry at the right hand of the Father, so it would not have done any good to have prayed in His Name.

But just before He went away, Jesus changed His disciples' way of praying. During the interim when the Old Covenant was going out, and the New Covenant was coming in, Jesus taught the disciples to pray what we call "The Lord's Prayer." He did not teach *us* to pray this way—did you ever stop to think about that? He taught His *disciples* to pray this way.

I did not say The Lord's Prayer isn't beautiful. I did not say we cannot learn something from it—because we can learn much from it. But where is the Name of Jesus in it? They didn't pray one thing in the Name of Jesus, did they? They didn't ask for one thing in the Name of Jesus, did they? *This is not the New Testament Church at prayer!* This is not the New Testament norm for prayer.

Right here in the 16th chapter of John is something we need to see: Just before He went away, Jesus changed their way of praying. *Under the New Covenant between God and the Church, we are to come to God by Jesus Christ.* (One reason we have missed a great deal is because we have tried to pray like they did back in the days of the Old Covenant.)

Notice that Jesus also said, *"ASK and ye SHALL RECEIVE, that your joy may be full."* Of course, this includes all prayer, but it includes praying for healing as well. How could your joy be full if your loved ones were home sick? That would be impossible, wouldn't it?

If we were getting more answers to prayer, we would have more joy. And if more of our joy were showing, we would get more people saved.

Healing is involved here. We have a right to ask for healing in the Name of Jesus. God does hear and answer prayer.

(3) Agree in prayer on the basis of Matthew 18:19.

> . . . if two of you shall agree on earth as touching any thing that they shall ask, it shall be done for them of my Father which is in heaven. For where two or three are gathered together IN MY NAME, there am I in the midst of them.
> —Matthew 18:19,20

Frequently we take the 20th verse out of its setting and apply it only to church services—but that really is not what it is talking about. You see, the 19th and 20th verses go together.

The 20th verse means: Wherever two people are, agreeing in prayer, Jesus is there to see that what they agreed on happens. Jesus is not talking about a church meeting here, although He *is* in church meetings.

Where two people are united and are demanding in Jesus' Name the healing of loved ones, their prayers are bound to be answered, because God watches over His Word to make it good.

The verse says "two of you on earth." Not two of you up in heaven. Just two. It brings it right down to where we are. And that word "anything" could include healing, couldn't it?

The two of you could be husband and wife. My wife and I have had marvelous answers to prayer agreeing together. People tell me "Brother Hagin, we *tried* that, and it didn't work." We didn't try—we *did* it! Jesus did not say if two would *try* to agree; He said to *do* it.

Sometimes we get into the natural and imagine, *Now, if we could get enough people—maybe a thousand—agreeing; maybe ten thousand praying, that would really get results!* That is human reasoning. God said that *two can get the job done.* Two is the most He ever mentions we need! He didn't say to get the whole church to agree on it (you couldn't get a whole church to agree on it to save your life). But if two of you agree, that's all it takes.

"*If two of you shall agree on earth as touching any thing . . . IT SHALL BE.*" Jesus did not say it might be. He did not say it is a possibility. "*IT SHALL BE DONE for them of my Father which is in heaven.*" Now that is either the truth or a lie, and I believe that Jesus told the truth!

Many times people come up to me after a service and ask me to agree with them in prayer for financial, physical, and spiritual needs.

I join hands with them and pray, "We are joining hands here physically to denote the fact that our spirits are agreeing. We agree that this need *is* met—not that it is going to be, because that is not faith, that would be future tense; that would be hope, not faith. We agree that the need is met, so we are praising God because we have agreed that it shall be done. By faith it is done right now, and we count it as done."

After praying like this, I open my eyes and say, "Brother (or Sister), is it done?"

Eight times out of ten they start bawling, "Brother Hagin, I sure *hope* it is."

I have to tell them, "It isn't. It isn't. I'm *believing* and you're *hoping.* There is no agreement here. It didn't work."

There is no use in our going around blaming God and casting reflections on the Bible if it didn't work. Friends, if it didn't work, *we* didn't work it—because Jesus Christ cannot lie. We must admit, "I didn't do it" and correct ourselves.

That is what a young Pentecostal evangelist did when he was dying of tuberculosis back in the early 1930s. He told me his story firsthand.

He had become bedfast and was hemorrhaging from both lungs. He had had to take his family to live on his father-in-law's farm.

One day his father-in-law was out in the fields plowing and his wife and mother-in-law were behind the house doing the wash.

This young evangelist begged God for enough strength to get out of bed and make it to a clump of trees and bushes a quarter of a mile down the road. He purposed in his heart, *I'm going to pray until I pray through and God heals me, or until they find me dead. One of the two.*

He reached the thicket and fell down exhausted. He couldn't have cried for help if he had wanted to. No one knew where he was.

"They'll never find you until the buzzards lead them to you," the devil assured him.

"Well," he said, "that's all right, devil. That's what I came out here to do. Just as soon as I can regain a little strength, I'm going to pray until I'm healed or die on the spot."

"Then, as I was lying there," he told me, "trying to muster enough strength to start praying, I got to thinking about it: Everywhere I had been, I had turned in prayer requests for my healing. *Hundreds* of people had prayed. *Thousands* of people had prayed. Every healing evangelist in America had laid hands on me. *Everybody* had prayed . . . .

"My, my. If you put all of those prayers together, it would be hundreds of hours of prayer. All these great men of faith had laid hands on me—and God uses healing evangelists.

"I decided: My God, I've missed it! I'm not going to pray at all. There is no use in my praying. I see where I've missed it. I shouldn't even have turned in those prayer requests. *I've been trying to get somebody else to pray. I've been trying to get God to give me what He says is already mine!*

"The Bible says I'm healed. Lord, I'm going to lie here flat on my back and praise You. I'm going to praise You until my healing is manifested."

He told me, "I just started whispering, 'Praise the Lord. Glory to God. Hallelujah. Thank You, Jesus.' After about 10 minutes of whispering 'Thank You, Jesus,' I got enough strength to lift my arms up by propping my elbows on the ground, and I praised God another 10 minutes or so. Then I got enough strength to lift my hands, and my voice got louder.

"And at the end of two hours, I was on my feet hollering 'Praise God' so loud somebody heard me several miles away."

You see—when he began to agree with what the Word of God said and acted on God's Word, he got results!

(4) Anoint with oil in accordance with James 5:14.

> Is any sick among you? let him call for the elders of the church; and let them pray over him, anointing him with oil in the name of the Lord: And the prayer of faith shall save the sick, and the Lord shall raise him up; and if he have committed sins, they shall be forgiven him.
>
> —James 5:14,15

First-century believers did not have a New Testament. They had some letters that could be passed around from church to church, but they did not have a Bible to study like we do.

They did not know that Peter had written by the Spirit of God "*by whose stripes ye WERE healed*" (1 Peter 2:24). But we know that.

If they could walk in health, how much more should we in this generation, with all the knowledge we have?

There really ought not be any sick among us—but "*is* any sick among you?" James is clearly talking to the church here, because he said, "let him call for the elders of the church."

Thank God, even if people have missed it and sinned, there is help for them. Notice James says, "if he has committed sins, they shall be forgiven him."

Too many times church people expect people who got saved on Sunday night to develop fully spiritually by Wednesday night—and they themselves didn't mature overnight.

No, they're just babes. The Bible teaches that there is a similarity between physical and spiritual growth: "*As newborn babes, desire the sincere milk of the word, that ye may grow thereby*" (1 Peter 2:2).

But we have been so foolish along this line—and God is going to hold us responsible. We ought to carry these spiritual babies on our faith, and we can as long as they really are bona fide spiritual babies.

Babies in the natural need to be cared for. They can't do anything for themselves. But because somebody loves them, they are fed, dressed, and cared for. If they are properly cared for, they will grow and respond.

Once I held a meeting for a pastor in Texas—and I'm ashamed that anybody in Texas would be as stupid as that poor fellow was.

I gave an invitation one Saturday night, and 39 people came and stood across the front. They included seven couples between 28 and 32 years of age. That's seven families. They had never been saved. They were noble prospects.

Afterwards, I asked the pastor, "Did you get those folks' names and addresses so you can follow up on them?"

"Aw, bless God," he said, "I believe if people got anything, they'll be back."

"I want to ask you a question," I said. "During this meeting, your daughter gave birth to a baby boy. Suppose you went to her house and said, 'I've come to see my boy. Where is he?' Would she say, 'Well, we thought if he were alive and well, he'd be in after a while'?"

And I said to that pastor, "My time is too valuable to hold a revival for an idiot. I'm closing tomorrow night." And I closed.

God is going to hold every church responsible for the babies born into the kingdom around its altars. When they backslide, we are ready to criticize them, yet we frequently are to blame for their backsliding.

That is what James is saying here. These people cannot act for themselves, so let them call for the *elders* of the church, and let them pray over them and anoint them with oil in the Name of the Lord, and if they have committed sins—even if they have missed it—they can get forgiveness for their sins and can get healed.

I often use this story as an illustration.

While I was shaving one morning, the Spirit of God spoke to me and said, "I want you to go to E.'s house because he has missed it, and he thinks now that because he has sinned, God doesn't love him anymore. He is not going to come back to church anymore."

I walked out to tell my wife—with lather still on my face— and I said, "Honey, before I go to the grocery store for you, I've got to go to E.'s. The Lord just said that he has missed it—he lost his temper and said a lot of things he shouldn't have—and the Lord told me to go out there and restore him."

I went back to finish shaving, and E.'s wife drove up. "Oh, Brother Hagin," she cried, "I want you to go see E. He lost his temper on the job yesterday and said a lot of things he shouldn't have. A back injury he had a long time ago has come back on him, and he's home in bed. He says he's not coming to church anymore. He believes God doesn't love him anymore because he sinned." She added, "Don't you tell him I came by here, because he won't like it."

"The Lord just spoke to me about it," I said. "You can ask my wife. I just got through telling her."

I went to their home, knocked on the door, and recognized E.'s voice saying, "Come in."

E. was so embarrassed that he pulled the covers up over his head. I could hear him crying. I got on my knees beside his bed, and I began to cry with him.

I pulled at the covers—he was holding on for dear life—and outpulled him. I simply took him in my arms. I said, "The Lord spoke to me and told me to come out here and restore you because you had missed it."

He began to cry again. He said, "Brother Hagin, something didn't go right on the job. I don't remember saying anything wrong, but some of them said I cursed. If I did, I don't know it. I told my wife, 'I'm not going to church anymore. The Lord doesn't love me.' "

I said, "Yes, He does. He loves you, and we love you, and He sent me out here to help you—and that *proves* He loves you. And we're not going to let the devil have you!"

He said, "My back is hurting me so bad!"

I laid my hand on his back and said, "Dear God, You love him. I know You do. You sent me out here to help him, and I want You to heal him right now and prove to him that You love him."

Suddenly he jumped like he had been shot, and he said, "It's all gone! It's all gone!"

Then he began to cry in a different way. He said, "The Lord *does* love me, doesn't He?"

I said, "Yes, He does."

And he came right on back to the Lord and right on back to church.

Well, the Lord sent me out there one more time—but he was only about a month old, and what do you expect of a one-month-old child?

I'm glad God has made provision for the babies. If you can't do it yourself, He has made provision for you where you can find help.

Is any sick among you? Go ahead and call for the elders of the church.

(5) Receive healing through the laying on of hands.

And he said unto them, Go ye into all the world, and preach the gospel to every creature. He that believeth and is baptized shall be saved; but he that believeth not shall be damned. And these signs shall follow them that believe; In my name shall they cast out devils; they shall speak with new tongues; They shall take up serpents; and if they drink any deadly thing, it shall not hurt them; they shall lay hands on the sick, and they shall recover.

—Mark 16:15-18 (The Great Commission)

When Jesus gave The Great Commission, He said, *"They shall lay hands on the sick, and they shall recover"* (v. 18). Laying hands on the sick is another method by which healing can be obtained. It belongs to the Church today.

Who can lay hands on people? All believers. All those who have believed the Gospel. Notice that our text says, *"them that believe . . . they shall lay hands on the sick"* (vv. 17,18).

The original Greek says, "*the believing ones* shall lay hands on the sick and they shall recover."

No, Jesus didn't say we were to *heal* the sick. We are to *lay hands on them* and *believe God*.

Every Christian can practice this. Parents should lay hands on their children if they are sick. A mother has a right to lay hands on her children if she is a believer. She shouldn't have to send for somebody else. We have the right to lay hands on one another. The Bible says, *"pray one for another, that ye may be healed"* (James 5:16).

We miss it sometimes trying to get God to move by just one method. We should get lined up with Him by listening to Him, seeing how He is leading at the moment, and then using whatever method He indicates.

I accidentally overheard one pastor tell another, "You ought to get Brother Hagin to come hold you a meeting. Since he's been to our church I haven't had half the sick calls I used to have.

"I don't mean that my people don't call me; I mean that they're getting their own healing. They're testifying in church about how they're praying and God is healing them. They're just thrilled."

Well, thank God, we can do something for ourselves. We can grow. When we learn to believe God and pray, we can go out and help others. But as long as we must depend on somebody else to pray and believe for us, we're going to be a liability instead of an asset.

Some people are not yet at the level where they can receive healing on their own, however. If you find yourself in this category, don't give up. Just come on a lower level of faith. Be one on whom hands are laid, and receive your healing this way. God wants to help you.

The Bible says, "they shall lay hands on *the sick*." It doesn't specify who the sick are; it just says they're sick. "These signs shall follow them that believe," the Scripture says. "They shall lay hands on the *sick*, and they shall recover."

Any believer can lay hands on the sick as their point of

contact. That is the point where you start believing that you receive your healing.

Many people ask me, "But Brother Hagin, what if I'm not healed?"

I reply, "If you *were* healed, you wouldn't have to believe it. If it were manifested, you would *know* it then, wouldn't you? But if you will take the step of believing that it is done, then you will receive it, because the principle of the prayer of faith is found in Mark 11:24:

> What things soever ye desire, when ye pray, believe that ye receive them, and ye shall have them.
> —Mark 11:24

Believe that you *receive* your healing, and what will happen? You will *have* it! You see, the *having* comes after the *believing*.

When I still was a young Baptist boy preacher—before I was baptized in the Holy Spirit—I woke up one Monday morning and half of my face was paralyzed. It wouldn't move.

I had been praying for myself because I didn't know anybody else to pray for me, but I found out that some people had built a church called the Full Gospel Tabernacle in our town, and these people believed in divine healing.

I said to myself, *I'll go down there Wednesday night and get that pastor to anoint me with oil.* The minute he anointed me and prayed, I lifted my hands and shouted, "Thank God, it is gone!"

I said it in faith. I knew what to say. I was Baptist—and I didn't know anything about the Holy Spirit—but I did know something about faith.

That was my point of contact when hands were laid on me. That was the point where I started believing "I receive my healing."

No, I did not feel healed.

No, I did not look healed.

But I was not going by looks or feeling. I was going by what I believed.

That's what a point of contact is: *It's the point when you release your faith and start believing for your healing.*

You must start somewhere. A man in a race would never run the race if he didn't get started. There has to be a starting place. Your starting place can be when hands are laid on you. That can be the place where you start believing: "I receive my healing."

People in the congregation began asking me, "Did the Lord really heal you, Kenneth?"

I said, "He sure did."

They said, "Well, you don't look healed. How do you feel?"

"Not any different."

"Well, if you don't *look* any different, and you don't *feel* healed, and we can *see* that you don't look healed, what makes you think you *are* healed?"

I said, "I don't *think* it; I *know* it."

You see, *faith is knowing.*

I've had people tell me, "I've got better sense than that."

And I tell them, "Well, you go ahead and do without healing. You notice my face is straight, don't you? I got it. I got my healing."

I knew what Jesus said was true. I knew that if I would believe that I received it, I would have it. I knew that if I really believed it, I would say that I believed it.

Not: I *will receive* it (future tense), but I *receive* it (present tense).

An associate pastor of a Full Gospel church in Tulsa was once sent to pray for a man in the church who was too sick to go to work.

He told me, "I had been hearing you preach, so I anointed him with oil, laid hands on him, and started my prayer when suddenly, without thinking, I stopped praying and said, 'What are you going to be doing tomorrow?'

"The sick man said, 'I'll be here in bed.'

" 'Well, there's no use finishing the prayer. I might as well leave now. You don't believe a thing,' I told him.

"The man thought about it a minute and said, 'That's right, isn't it?'

"I asked him, 'When are you going to get healed?'

" 'Why,' he said, 'when you anoint me with oil—when you lay hands on me and pray—that's when.'

"This man turned to his wife and said—even before I finished that prayer—'Call the boss and tell him I'll be on the job tomorrow.'

"Then I prayed for him," the pastor said, "and bless God, he was on the job the next day."

A woman once ran up to the pastor and me on the platform and said, "Brother Pastor, Brother Hagin, pray for me right now."

The pastor said, "Well, we're having a healing service after a while. I'm going to preach a healing message and Brother Hagin is going to lay hands on all the sick at the close of the service. It won't be long." The singing had already started.

"Yes, yes," she said, "but I want you and Brother Hagin to lay hands on me *now*, because I'm going home and go to bed!"

What good would it have done to have laid hands on her and prayed? She had already confessed it won't work.

When you *pray*, the Bible says, *believe* that you *receive* and you *shall have*. The laying on of hands is the point of contact to release your faith. That's when you start believing.

I lay hands on people as their point of contact. But there is another spiritual law that also can bring about their healing. That is the Law of Contact and Transmission.

One can be anointed, as God wills, with healing power to minister healing. And *when that person lays hands on the sick in obedience to this spiritual law, the contact of those anointed hands will transmit God's healing power to the sick.*

The believer also has to exercise faith for this Law of Contact and Transmission to work. The woman with the issue of blood (Matthew 9) is an example of this.

Jesus was anointed with healing power, and the Bible says that power went out of Him and healed her. But Jesus said, *"Daughter, be of good comfort; thy faith hath made thee whole"* (v. 22).

I lay hands on the sick not only as a point of contact, but also in obedience to this Law of Contact and Transmission so that the contact of my hands will transmit God's healing power to undo that which Satan has wrought and to effect a healing and a cure.

Why do I speak so boldly about it?

Because the Lord Jesus Christ Himself appeared to me in a vision. He laid the finger of His right hand in the palms of both of my hands and said, "I have called you and have anointed you, and I have given unto you a special anointing to minister to the sick. Be bold about it.

"Tell the people that you saw Me. Tell them exactly what I have told you. Tell them that I told you to tell them, and if they will believe that you are anointed and they will receive that anointing, then power will flow from your hands to their bodies, will effect a healing and a cure in their bodies, and will drive out their sickness and their disease. And the bolder you are to tell it, the more results you will have."

(6)   Receive healings through gifts of healings.

First Corinthians 12:9 says that one of the spiritual gifts God has placed in the Church is gifts of healings—which is separate from the other methods to obtain healing.

What is "gifts of healings"? It is a supernatural mani-festation of healing power through one individual to another. That is the simplest way to state it.

Anything we get from God is a gift. Therefore, generally speaking, any healing would be a gift. But that is not a manifestation of the "gifts of healings." Manifestations of the gifts of healings are initiated by the Holy Spirit.

After I was baptized in the Holy Spirit, I still did not understand the Spirit of God. All I knew was that I was filled with the Holy Spirit.

After I received "the left foot of fellowship" from among the Baptists, I aligned myself with one of the Full Gospel groups, and accepted the pastorate of a small church in North Texas. That is where I met and married my lovely wife. She was a Methodist, and she had not been baptized in the Holy Spirit, but she believed in it.

The fourth night after we were married, as we were having family prayer together in her good old Methodist home, the Lord through the Spirit said to me, "Lay your hands on your wife and I'll fill her with the Holy Spirit."

This was 1938, and I was new in these things. I had received the Holy Spirit in 1937. I had never seen anybody lay hands on someone to receive the baptism in the Holy Spirit. They didn't do it that way in the circles I operated in, and I didn't know if that was right or not. I thought, *Maybe if I ignore it, it will go away.* But it did not go away.

Again He said, "Lay your hands on your wife and I'll fill her with the Holy Spirit." I recognized it was the Lord Jesus speaking to my spirit through the Holy Spirit, but I didn't want to do anything wrong.

Then at midnight (I looked at my watch) on the 28th day of November 1938, that same voice repeated, "Lay your hands on your wife and I'll fill her with the Holy Spirit."

I opened my eyes and looked around half scared. I said to myself, *Well, it wouldn't hurt to try it!* I laid my left hand on my wife's head and instantly she lifted both hands and started talking in tongues. She talked an hour and a half in other tongues and sang three songs in tongues. We had Pentecost in that good old Methodist home!

Then, the same voice told me what to do and what to tell my mother-in-law for her healing. She was going into the hospital the next day to be operated on for a double goiter. She didn't have any faith for healing; you don't have your suitcase packed ready to go to the hospital if you're expecting to be healed. The voice told me, "I have given you gifts of healings and have sent you to minister to the sick."

When I did what the Spirit of God had told me, instantly the part of the goiter that you could see went down like someone had stuck a pin in a balloon.

She was not healed because she believed God. If you had questioned her afterwards, she would have said, "No, no. I know it wasn't my faith. I couldn't have had faith for a thing like that."

Do you know why she was healed? Because the Spirit of God told me what to do.

The manifestation of the gifts of healings does not work as I will, however; it works as the Spirit wills. I have pushed every button, pulled every lever, said everything that I've said before in the same places—and nothing has happened.

Then I've gone along with nothing happening and I've said, "It's never going to happen again." And it will start working. You see, the manifestation of the Spirit is as the Spirit wills. Thank God for these manifestations. I believe in them.

But that is only one way to obtain healing. The best method of all is simply to know First Peter 2:24, *"by whose stripes ye were healed."* (Not *going to be—were* healed.)

(7)   Know that healing belongs to you.

The best method by which you can be healed is to know for yourself from our text Scriptures (Isaiah 53:4,5, Matthew 8:17, and First Peter 2:24) that healing is in God's redemptive plan; it belongs to you; and by His stripes *we are healed.*

We refuse to allow disease or sickness in our bodies, because we ARE healed. We know that the pain, sickness, or disease that seems to be in our bodies was laid on Jesus. He bore it. We do not need to bear it. All we need to do is agree with God and His Word and accept the fact that *"himself took our infirmities, and bare our sicknesses"* and *"with his stripes we are healed."*

We simply *know* it, so we thank God. We don't have to have anybody lay hands on us. We don't have to have any manifestation of the gifts of the Spirit. We simply thank the Father for our perfect deliverance.

All believers should thoroughly understand that their healing was consummated in Christ. When they come to know that in their spirits—just as they know it in their heads—that will be the end of sickness and disease in their bodies.

But all believers do not thoroughly understand that acting on the Scriptures is a method of receiving divine healing. All believers have not been taught it. This truth has not been preached as it should even among those who supposedly believe in divine healing. Therefore, believers' information is slight in this area, and you cannot operate and believe beyond knowledge.

That is why God has provided these seven methods by which believers can be healed through the Word.

(Another exposition of this subject can be found in my lesson entitled "7 Methods of Obtaining Healing Through the Word.")

5. Know the difference between God's initiating healings supernaturally and man's initiating healings through his own faith.

5. Know the difference between God's initiating healings supernaturally and man's initiating healings through his own faith.

We need to know the difference; otherwise, we may be hindered.

In John's Gospel the 5th chapter we read about the pool called Bethesda in Jerusalem. Five porches had been built around that pool. They were thronged with sick people—the crippled, halt, maimed, blind—waiting for the troubling of the waters.

An angel came down from heaven at a certain season and troubled the waters. When that happened, the first person in the pool got healed.

You see, God initiated something on His own. He is a sovereign being. If He wanted to send an angel down there by an act of His divine sovereignty, trouble the waters, and heal somebody that way, He could. He didn't have to write to someone on earth to endorse it!

People were getting healed there. They wouldn't have been there if they hadn't been.

I don't see sick people being carried into some churches on stretchers, do you? I've gone to some places and never seen any sick people. Why? Because nobody was getting healed there! But I've gone to other places where things were happening, and the sick were there.

Did you notice that just *one* person got healed at the pool? The first one in was the only one healed. Then the crowd had to wait until the next troubling of the waters.

The gifts of healings operate in a similar manner. Have you ever been in a crowd of 5,000 or more, yet only 15 to 20 people were healed through special manifestations of the word of knowledge, revelation gifts, and gifts of healings? (These special manifestations often operate together.) Seeing these healings, other people start believing God and they get healed, too.

So God does initiate some things on His own. Thank God for that. I love that. He uses me in special manifestations in a limited measure, although that is not my main ministry.

I often have been awakened during the night and have realized that it was the Lord who awakened me. "Lord, I don't know how to pray as I ought. You help me," I have said. The Holy Spirit began to help me, and I began to pray aloud in other tongues, just lying there in bed beside my wife, never awakening her.

I've prayed that way thousands of times through these many, many years. Occasionally when I would finish, I would have a vision. I would see my service the next night. I would see myself point to a person, and I would hear myself say, "I saw you last night in a vision in my room. You have . . . . " (I would name what was wrong with them physically, and I would tell them they were healed).

That was the gifts of healings in operation. These people would be healed instantly; not one ever failed to be healed. You see, God had initiated something on His own. Such manifestations are signs of His presence and His power.

Some people go to a service and wait for such a manifestation. Many dear people would never be healed if God didn't initiate something! But—many die while they are waiting for something like that to happen to them.

You need to know this: *Although God does move this way, it does not always work for everybody, and it never will.*

My wife and I, as pastors, have visited people who were on their deathbeds. We prayed for them—we believe in that—and we have seen people healed in answer to our prayers. But sometimes God will initiate something on His own.

I am thinking of one woman. Just as I started to pray, the voice of the Lord came to me and said, "Don't pray. Tell her to get up. She's healed."

Isn't that a silly thing to do? Here she is on her deathbed. I said, "Sister, I never told anybody this before, but the Lord told me to tell you to get up—you're healed!" She got up and was healed.

That was on Thursday. On Sunday she was jumping and shouting in our church, giving her testimony at both services.

A woman in the church said, "Brother Hagin, there is a woman over in our end of town who has been given up to die and is bedfast. If you healed this woman, would you come over and heal this other woman?"

I said, "No, ma'am. If they wanted me to come—if they called for me—I would go. But God is a gentleman, and I am a gentleman. I am not going to force my way in on anybody. You see, this woman who was healed asked me to come. Her neighbor had told her how the Lord used me sometimes and said if I would come, she would be healed. And she was, because she believed. God initiated something on His own."

Jesus did not say to go into all the world and *prove* to people that divine healing is so. He said, "Go *preach* the Word."

Once when I was preaching in Oklahoma, some people put an advertisement in the newspaper offering a $1,000 reward for proof that anybody was getting healed in my services.

These people also wrote me letters challenging me to debate, and they went on the radio and made a lot of outlandish statements about divine healing.

I just ignored them. I don't pay any attention to a donkey's braying. (I had heard them bray before. It was nothing new to me.)

One night as I stepped on the platform, I saw five well-dressed men standing in the back. The voice of the Lord said to me, "Those five men are so-called ministers from such-and-such a church. They are the ones challenging you. Now I want you to take such-and-such a text and preach a sermon." I opened my Bible and took off.

The pastor said afterwards, "I thought you were going to quote the whole New Testament!" You talk about a fellow preaching—I never preached like that before or since!

As I came to the close of my sermon, that same voice said to my spirit (not my ears), "Now demonstrate to the congregation what you preached."

"Oh, I like it when the Spirit moves on me like that. I wish He would do it every service, but He doesn't. It is as *He* wills, not as *I* will.

You see, there was a man lying there on a stretcher. Anyone could have seen that he was nearly dead. He was just a skeleton with skin stretched over it. He looked like a corpse—the picture of death.

There also were two young ladies in the service that night who were just about to be graduated from high school with honors. They had been saved a few nights before.

The Word of the Lord came unto me, saying, "Say thou unto this congregation, son of man: 'I am going to lay my hands on these two young ladies, and each one will receive the Holy Spirit and begin to speak with other tongues. Then I am going to walk down there and not touch that man or pray for him. I am going to speak to him and tell him to rise, and he will rise up off that stretcher and be healed. He will walk across the front of this church, and every person in this church will see him instantly healed before his eyes. And if any of these things do not happen, then I am a false prophet.' "

That is what He told me to say. That puts you on the spot!

But if it happens—which it will—it is a sign. God sometimes does some things for signs. He initiates them on His own.

The Bible says, "many signs and wonders" were wrought by the hands of the apostles (Acts 5:12). What were they? We don't know.

I concluded, "This is a sign unto you that the Spirit of God is upon me; that He has called me and has anointed me into such a ministry."

I called the young ladies forward, and as I put my hands upon the first I said, "Receive the Holy Spirit." She lifted her hands and began speaking with other tongues. I held the microphone in front of her. She did not stammer. She did not stutter. She spoke a language.

I said, "Now listen to that. She is not all worked up. She is just standing here calmly speaking with tongues. A little child would know that is a language!"

I laid hands on the other girl and said, "Be filled with the Holy Spirit." She calmly started speaking in tongues.

Then I walked down to the fellow on the stretcher, spoke to him, and he got up and walked right there in front of everybody.

"Well, why don't you do that every service?" you might ask.

I didn't do it then! The Holy Spirit did it through me.

"Well, why doesn't *He* do it every service?"

I don't know. If you want to know, go ask Him. He's the One who did it.

I long for these manifestations if they do not occur occasionally, and I thank God for them whether they are manifested through me or somebody else. But brother and sister, I get just as thrilled when the word of faith is preached.

You need to realize, as the story of the woman with the issue of blood tells us, that *your own faith can initiate healing.* YOUR faith can do it! You don't have to wait for God to move.

You see, this woman had spent all of her living and had suffered many things of many physicians, but grew worse, the Bible says.

When she heard of Jesus, she got in the crowd behind Him

and touched His robe, for she had said, *"If I may touch but his clothes, I shall be whole"* (Mark 5:28).

Immediately "the fountain of her blood was dried up" and Jesus turned to her and said, *"Daughter, THY FAITH hath made thee whole"* (v. 34).

"I did not initiate your healing. It was not some kind of a special manifestation. YOUR FAITH made you whole. YOUR FAITH did it." Oh, I get thrilled with that!

I remember that is what He said to me when I was on the bed of sickness: "If *her faith* made *her* whole, *your faith* can make *you* whole." And *my faith* made *me* whole!

That is the reason I want so desperately to get this faith message across to humanity. I know what it did for me as a 16-year-old Baptist boy.

"You've got to die—got to die. You can't live," medical doctors told me. Thank God for doctors. I appreciated everything they could do for me. They were so kind.

After I was healed, I went to Dr. Robason's office to thank him. I said, "Doc, I appreciate you. You're the only one who told me what was wrong with me. You're the only one who told me there was nothing that could be done for me and to stay ready to go."

He wept and said, "This is a miracle of God. Medical science could not help you. I believe in telling people the truth."

I said, "I appreciate that, sir."

He never charged us anything. He said, "I can't do anything, but I'll come day or night, son, if you want me to. Just have them call me, and I'll come. It will never cost you a penny."

I believe God will bless a man like that for wanting to help people and for telling them the truth. I appreciated that dear man. He's up in heaven now, thank God.

But I tell you: MY FAITH WORKED. I KNOW IT WORKS. AND FAITH WORKS TODAY.

6. Healing is not always instant. Sometimes it is gradual.

6. Healing is not always instant. Sometimes it is gradual.

By not realizing this, sometimes we make a mistake and lose out with God.

Someone once said to me, "Brother Hagin, in Bible days, people always got healed instantly."

I replied, "What about the 10 lepers? The Bible says that they were healed *as they went*" (Luke 17:14).

A woman wrote me, "I came in your prayer line 10 months ago. When you laid hands on me, I fell under the power, but I didn't feel any different. I had had a stroke that left me with no feeling in my left arm and leg, and I had to get around with the help of a crutch.

"I guess people didn't think I got healed, because I still was on that crutch when I left the meeting. When I got about two blocks from the church, suddenly a warm glow came through my leg and feeling was restored to my arm and leg. Now both are all right.

"Not only that," she continued, "but I had smoked cigarettes for 40 years. I knew it was wrong, and I wanted to quit, but I couldn't. You know, I haven't smoked another cigarette since you prayed for me. I haven't even *wanted* one."

Glory to God, the power of God did that. You can't always tell at the time what has happened.

Another example is a woman who wrote me several months after we had held a radio rally in Texas. An arthritis victim, she, too, walked with the aid of a crutch, and she did not get her healing instantly after prayer.

She said, "I got back on my crutch, went back to the book table, then went to my car, laid the books up on top of it, and was fumbling in my purse for my keys when suddenly I realized: *I'm healed!* The manifestation came when I was standing beside the car. Two months have come and gone and I have not had to use my crutch any more. I'm healed, and I want to thank you."

The 10 lepers were healed as they went. The Bible also says that under the ministry of Jesus, the nobleman's son "began to amend" from the hour Jesus prayed for him (John 4). What does that mean? It means that he began to get better from the hour he was ministered to until he was healed.

The Bible says, "they shall lay hands on the sick, and they *shall recover*" (Mark 16:18). Sometimes it works that way. We need to know that healing is not always instant. When it is instant, thank God for it, but sometimes it is gradual.

Dr. John Lake said that sometimes instant healings are a curse, because some people get healed, go away, and forget God. He believed that people who are gradually healed can see that they get better and better as they walk in God, and that knowledge becomes of invaluable wealth to them.

7. God's method of healing is spiritual, and it can be lost.

7. God's method of healing is spiritual, and it can be lost.

Divine healing is not "*mental*," as Christian Science, Unity, and other metaphysical teachers claim. Neither is it *physical*, as the medical world teaches. When God heals, He heals through the *spirit*. God is not a *mind*. God is not a *man*. God is a *Spirit*.

Being healed by the power of God is being healed by the Spirit of God. And because divine healing is spiritual, it can be lost. Many people have lost their healing by opening the door to the devil.

It is a remarkable fact that when Jesus came on the scene as a healer, He demanded faith—and faith is born of the spirit. All of Jesus' healings were spiritual.

One man said to me, "I believe if God heals you, you are healed forever."

"Well," I said, "that can't be true, because when Jesus Himself appeared in a vision to John on the island of Patmos and sent a message to the seven churches in Asia Minor, He said to one of them, '*hold that fast which thou hast*' (Rev. 3:11). Why did He want to tell them to hold onto it, if they couldn't lose it?"

This man said, "Maybe I'm wrong."

I said, "I know you're wrong. That's the reason you've lost your healing. Your wrong thinking has opened the door to the devil to put your sickness back on you. When I ministered to you eight months ago, were you healed?"

"Yes."

"Have you had any symptoms in these eight months—any pain?"

"Not a pain. Not a symptom."

"I want to ask you a question, then: How long had you had this ailment before I laid hands on you?"

"Twenty-five years," he said. (He was a man more than 60 years of age.)

I said, "In all those 25 years, was there ever a day when you were without pain?"

"Not one day."

"Was there ever a day when you were without symptoms?"

"Not one day. I took medicine every day for 25 years."

"I laid hands on you in the Name of Jesus eight months ago, and every symptom and pain disappeared for eight solid months."

He said, "That's right."

"Why, dear brother," I said, "a child would know he was healed. But because your sickness has come back on you, you are saying the Lord never did heal you.

"I'll tell you exactly what happened. When the first symptom—the first pain—returned, you said, 'I thought I was healed. I guess I'm not.'"

Do you know what this man had the audacity to say? His eyes got big and he said to me, "Why, you must be a mindreader or a fortune teller! That's exactly what happened!"

"No," I said, "I'm not reading your mind or telling your fortune. I knew you had to open the door for the devil to come back in."

"But that's exactly what I said. That's exactly what I did," he said.

I told him, "When you said, 'I thought I was healed. I guess I'm not,' you opened the door consciously or unconsciously (it's still open) and you said, 'Come back in, Mr. Devil, and put it back on me!' And he obliged you."

I talked to that man for 45 minutes. I preached to him, taught him, and laid hands on him in the middle of a cow pasture. Bless God, he got his healing, and this time he kept it.

I saw him years later, and he was still healed, because he had learned how to keep it. He had learned how to resist the devil. He had learned how to resist the symptoms by saying, "No, devil, you're not going to put that back on me. I'm healed and I know I am—and I'm holding onto it."

P.C. "Dad" Nelson, the late faith preacher who established Southwestern Assemblies of God College, was a well-educated Baptist pastor. He said, "More people lose their healing over a counterattack than any other one thing."

That is scriptural. It is a principle that the devil is always going to try to come back in where he has been. And if you let him, he'll come in and put the same sickness or disease, the same symptoms, or something worse on you—if you allow it. That is why we need to know that because healing is spiritual, it can be lost.

How can you keep your healing? *"Resist the devil, and he will flee from you"* (James 4:7). That means resist everything that is of the devil.

If the suggestion to steal or lie came to you and you resisted, you would be resisting the devil, wouldn't you? By the same token, when you resist anything that is of the devil, you are resisting the devil.

The Bible said, *"For God hath not given us the spirit of fear; but of power, and of love, and of a sound mind"* (2 Tim. 1:7). If God did not give us the spirit of fear (did you notice He calls it a spirit?), who gave it to us? If it is a spirit, it had to come from another source. It's of the devil. *Fear is of the devil.*

I started practicing this life of faith more than 40 years ago as a Baptist boy preacher. If fear came, I spoke to it. I said, "Fear,

I resist you in the Name of Jesus. I refuse to fear." I learned that if I would stand my ground, it always would leave. Sometimes I would have to stand there and resist it for a day or two, but eventually it would go. Fear has been gone for so many years that I do not know what it means to have fear.

Then, if doubt came in, I spoke to it, too. I said, "Doubt, I resist you. I refuse to doubt."

My head said, "Boy, you're already doubting."

"What do you mean?" I said. "No, I'm not. It's not in my heart; it's just in my head. The devil put it there, and I'm not walking by my head anyway! I refuse to doubt."

Then, if sickness came, I spoke to it. I said, "Sickness, I resist you." (That's resisting the devil, as we proved, for *sickness is of the devil*. He is the author of it, and to resist sickness is to resist the devil.)

I also have successfully resisted the flu all these years. The longest any symptoms ever stayed was an hour and a half.

Generally speaking, we Christians do not do that. At the first little symptom of flu that shows up—a headache or whatever—we will say, "Oh, yes, I've got it. Yeah, I knew I'd get it. I knew I'd be the first one. You all pray for me."

Well, it won't do any good to pray for you. You've already confessed, "It's mine. I've got it."

After I got baptized with the Holy Spirit and went among Full Gospel people, I knew more about faith than they did. (They knew more about the Holy Spirit than I did.) I learned from them about the Holy Spirit and I tried to help them on faith, but I couldn't help too many of them.

They told me it wouldn't last. They talked about being *up* and *down*, *in* and *out*, in the *valley* today and on the *mountaintop* tomorrow. I didn't know what they were talking about.

"Well, *you'll* come down," they said. Forty-five years have come and gone, and I haven't come down yet! I've never been in the valley yet. I'm still on the mountain—the mountain of victory. If I go down in the valley—like Fred Price says—I'll go down to rescue somebody else.

When I was pastoring my first Full Gospel church, we had fellowship meetings the first Monday of the month. The pastors all lined up and talked about their troubles, bless their hearts. I did my best to help them. I wept over it because I couldn't.

I would come along and they would say with long faces, "How goes the *battle*?" (They were all in a battle.) I would wave and grin, and say, "Boys, it couldn't be better. I don't have a care." I would go on by. I didn't want to get contaminated with their unbelief. That stuff will rub off on you.

Some people get all built up in faith in a service and then go back among a bunch of unbelief, get down and out, and say, "That will work for Brother Hagin because he's a preacher and God has given him the gift of faith, but it just doesn't work for me."

God's Word will work for everybody.

You see, I was walking by faith, and those other preachers were walking by sight. Certainly, I had problems in the church, but I had already told the Lord, "Lord, I'm just the under-shepherd. You're the Great Shepherd of the sheep. I know what my job is. I'm going to preach the Word. I'm going to visit the people who need visiting. I'm going to treat everybody alike—and I'm going to turn the rest of it over to you, because I don't know what to do, anyway. I'm just 21 years old."

I plainly said to the Lord, "Lord, it's Yours. I'm not going to worry about it. I'm not going to miss one meal or lose one wink of sleep." And I didn't.

God straightened everything out. You see, I had a "trouble" church. I didn't know it at first because I was new in Full Gospel circles. Nobody would take this church. It had been in existence 23 years and had never supported a pastor until I came. Yet it was the fourth largest church in that area! When I left, 40 preachers put in their applications for it, but when I took it, nobody else would have it.

God told me to take it. Glory to God, faith works! *Faith works in every avenue of your life.*

I was preaching for the Full Gospel Business Men in St.

Louis in 1971, when a Massachusetts couple stopped me in the hotel lobby and told me how their 15-year-old son had been healed of an incurable disease at a Full Gospel Business Men's convention the previous year.

They had been taking him to specialists in New York City every few months. Friends invited the family to the Full Gospel sessions. They heard me teach on making a confession of faith. The parents wondered if it would work.

The next day when they asked their son how he was feeling, he said, "I was healed yesterday."

"Are you sure?" they asked.

"Oh, yes. I never was more sure of anything in my life," he replied.

"But how are you *feeling*?" they inquired.

"That's unimportant. The Word of God says I'm healed."

That boy got hold of it!

Every time his parents asked him how he was, the boy answered, "I'm fine."

Finally the time came for his next checkup in New York City. The doctors were puzzled. They asked to keep him for three days to run tests. Every test proved negative. "We know it's incurable, and we know he had it, but he doesn't have it any more," the doctors concluded.

In one of my meetings the pastor came forward for healing. I said, "Are you healed?"

He poked his stomach. "No. No, I didn't get it," he said. "It's still sore. I didn't get it."

At the same time, a 72-year-old man whose sense of balance was impaired was helped to the front by his daughter. He staggered like a drunk without his cane, and the doctors said he soon would be confined to a wheelchair. He had hearing aids in both ears—he couldn't have heard thunder without them—and he also was facing major surgery.

He was instantly healed. He heard a pocket watch tick; he talked to people in normal tones; and he walked a straight line without his cane. I saw him 10 years later when he was 82. No hearing aids. No cane. He had never had the operation. He had never had any more pain or symptoms. At 82 he was walking straight, talking normally, and living a full life.

His pastor was in the same service. He told me, "Brother Hagin, I had to resign my church. I was just 56 years old. I ought to be preaching still, I know, but these last 10 years have been so much worse. I just can't carry on. I wish you could help me."

I said, "I can't. God can't. Nobody can. You won't let them."

He said, "I've heard you preach, but I'll tell you, I'm not going to believe that I've got something when my physical senses tell me I don't have it!"

I said, "You go sit down and do without your healing, brother, because you'll never get it."

I didn't mean to be nasty, but it was the truth. And he never got healed. He missed it. Do you see what he was doing? He was walking by the physical senses. If he couldn't *feel* healed, he wouldn't believe he *was* healed.

Physical senses build life fences. They fence God out and fence a person, his sickness, and the devil in.

Are you healed? How do you know you are? The Word says so.

How do you know you are?

Because Matthew 8:17 says, *"Himself took my infirmities, and bare my sicknesses"* and First Peter 2:24 says, *"by whose stripes ye were healed."*